IQ
Puzzles 2

Pocket**Puzzles**

Capella

This edition published in 2007 by Arcturus Publishing Limited
26/27 Bickels Yard, 151–153 Bermondsey Street,
London SE1 3HA

In Canada published for Indigo Books
468 King St W,
Suite 500,
Toronto,
Ontario M5V 1L8

ISBN: 1-84193-602-2
ISBN: 978-1-84193-602-4

Printed in China

Contents

Domino Placement

A standard set of twenty-eight dominoes has been laid out as shown. Can you draw in the edges of them all? The check-box is provided as an aid, so that you can see which dominoes have been located.

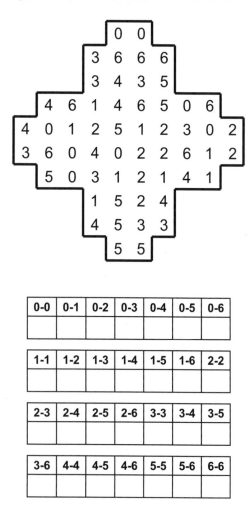

0-0	0-1	0-2	0-3	0-4	0-5	0-6

1-1	1-2	1-3	1-4	1-5	1-6	2-2

2-3	2-4	2-5	2-6	3-3	3-4	3-5

3-6	4-4	4-5	4-6	5-5	5-6	6-6

Hexagony

Can you place the hexagons into the grid, so that where any hexagon touches another along a straight line, the contents of both triangles is the same? No rotation of any hexagon is allowed!

Simple as A, B, C?

Each of the small squares in the grid below contains either A, B or C. Every row, column and each of the two long diagonals has exactly two of each letter. The information in the clues refers only to the squares in that row or column. To help you solve this problem, we have provided as many clues as we think you will need! Can you tell the letter in each square?

Across

1 One A is directly next to and left of a B. The other A is directly next to and right of a B.

2 No two squares containing the same letter are adjacent.

3 The Cs are between the As.

5 Neither of the two squares at either end of the row contains a C.

Down

1 The Bs are higher than the As.

2 The As are higher than the Cs.

3 Each C is directly next to and below an A.

4 The As are in adjacent squares.

5 The As are higher than the Bs.

6 The Cs are between the Bs.

	1	2	3	4	5	6
1						
2						
3						
4						
5						
6						

Total Concentration

The blank squares below should be filled with whole numbers between 1 and 40 inclusive, any of which may occur more than once, or not at all.

The numbers in every horizontal row add up to the totals on the right, as do the two long diagonal lines; whilst those in every vertical column add up to the totals along the bottom.

Can you discover the missing numbers?

								176
	40	6				21		203
18			4	11	16	9	13	97
24	8	1	8	38	10	12		138
19	35	33	27		25	14	4	160
38	29		34	6	19	15		202
15	25	34	33		12	38	29	220
	36	5	30	12	13	31	22	188
10	30	38	2		16			147
190	215	164	157	174	126	150	179	122

7

Shape Up

Every row and column in this grid originally contained one circle, one diamond, one square, one triangle and two blank squares, although not necessarily in that order.

Every symbol with a black arrow refers to the first of the four symbols encountered when travelling in the direction of the arrow. Every symbol with a white arrow refers to the second of the four symbols encountered in the direction of the arrow.

Can you complete the original grid?

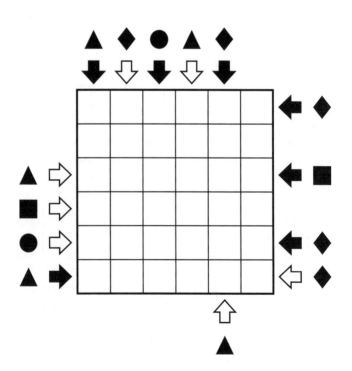

Mind Over Matter

Given that the letters are valued 1-26 according to their places in the alphabet, can you crack the mystery code to reveal the missing letter?

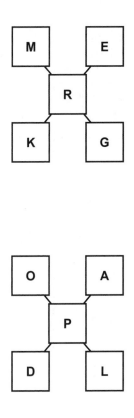

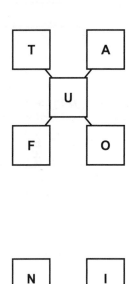

Whatever Next?

Which of the four lettered alternatives (A, B, C or D) fits most logically into the empty square?

64	8	36
100	25	512
27	125	81

16	49	216
121	8	4
144	81	169

25	216	64
81	49	100
121	9	4

~~~~~~

15	86	120
42	38	66
200	48	6

A

32	19	94
14	17	152
68	44	48

B

56	77	13
98	45	84
116	40	24

C

169	512	27
100	8	64
36	9	25

D

The Bottom Line

Can you fill each square in the bottom line with the correct digit?

Every square in the solution contains only one digit from each of the lettered lines above, although two or more squares in the solution may contain the same digit.

At the end of every row is a score, which shows:

a the number of digits placed in the correct finishing position on the bottom line, as indicated by a tick; and

b the number of digits which appear on the bottom line, but in a different position, as indicated by a cross.

SCORE

A	1	2	3	4	✓ ✗
B	5	6	1	3	✓ ✗
C	6	4	2	7	✓ ✗
D	7	3	1	8	✓ ✗
E	2	5	8	4	✓ ✗
					✓✓✓✓

Combiku

Each horizontal row and vertical column should contain different shapes and different numbers.

Every square will contain one number and one shape and no combination may be repeated anywhere else in the puzzle; so, for instance, if a square contains a 3 and a star, then no other square containing a 3 will also contain a star and no other square with a star will contain a 3.

Ls in Place

Twelve L-shapes like the ones here need to be inserted in the grid and each L has one hole in it.

There are three pieces of each of the four kinds shown here and any piece may be turned or flipped over before being put in the grid. No pieces of the same kind touch, even at a corner.

The pieces fit together so well that you cannot see any spaces between them; only the holes show. Can you tell where the Ls are?

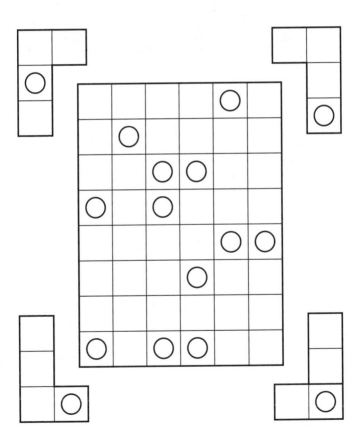

Box Clever

When the box below is folded to form a cube, just one of the five options (A, B, C, D or E) can be produced. Which?

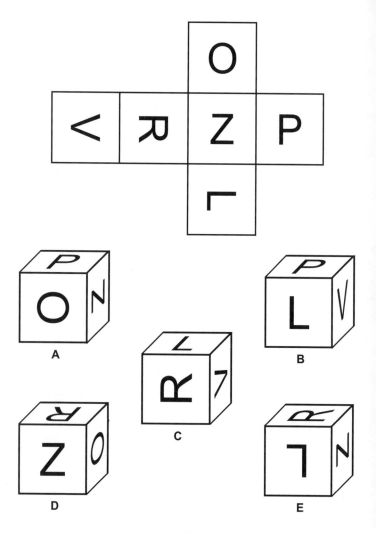

A

B

C

D

E

Latin Square

The grid should be filled with numbers from 1 to 6, so that each number appears just once in every row and column. The clues refer to the digit totals in the squares, eg A 1 2 3 = 6 means that the numbers in squares A1, A2 and A3 add up to 6.

1. D 1 2 = 7
2. E 2 3 4 = 13
3. F 1 2 3 = 6
4. B C 1 = 10
5. A B 2 = 3
6. C D 3 = 8
7. A B 4 = 9
8. D E 5 = 11
9. D E 6 = 3
10. A 5 6 = 4
11. B 5 6 = 7

	A	B	C	D	E	F
1						
2						
3						
4						
5						
6						

Symbolism

Each of these squares should contain one or more symbols from the numbered square to the left of its particular horizontal row, plus one or more symbols from the lettered square above its particular vertical column. However, one square doesn't follow this rule. Which is the odd one out?

	A	B	C	D	E	F
	◄ ≈	♣ $	‡ ¿	♦ #	♪ ¶	Σ ☼
1 ∩ π	◄ ∩ π	∩ $	‡ ¿ π ∩	∩ ♦ π	∩ ¶ π	Σ ∩ ☼
2 ♠ ß	≈ ♠ ß	♣ $ ß	ß ♠ ‡	♦ ♠ ß	♠ ¶	ß Σ ♠
3 £ ▶	◄ ≈ ▶	£ ▶ $	▶ ¿	£ #	♪ ▶ £	☼ ▶
4 Ω §	Ω §	≈ Ω $ ♣	¿ Ω §	§ Ω ♦	♪ ¶	§ Ω Σ
5 △ ♥	△ ♥	◄ ♥	△ ‡	# ♦ ♥	¶ ♪ △	△ Σ ♥
6 ▲ ♪	◄ ♪ ▲	♪ ▲ ♣	‡ ▲	♪ ▲ #	♪ ♪ ▲	▲ ♪ ☼
7 ▼ φ	≈ φ	♣ ▼ φ	φ ▼ ¿	▼ ♦ #	φ ¶	φ Σ ▼

Battleships

Can you place the vessels into the diagram? Some parts of vessels or sea squares have already been filled in. A number to the right or below a row or column refers to the number of occupied squares in that row or column.

Any vessel may be positioned horizontally or vertically, but no part of a vessel touches part of any other vessel, either horizontally, vertically or diagonally.

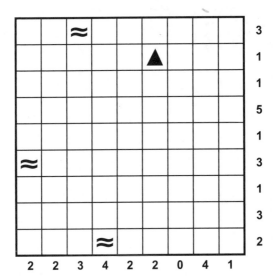

Empty Area of Sea: ≈

Aircraft Carrier: ◀■■▶

Battleships: ◀■▶ ◀■▶

Cruisers: ◀▶ ◀▶ ◀▶

Submarines: ● ● ● ●

		≈							3
					▲				1
									1
									5
									1
≈									3
									1
									3
			≈						2
2	2	3	4	2	2	0	4	1	

Coin Collecting

In this puzzle, an amateur coin collector has been out with his metal detector, searching for booty. He didn't have time to dig up all the coins he found, so has made a grid map, showing their locations, in the hope that if he loses the map, at least no-one else will understand it... However, he didn't count on YOU coming across the strange grid (as seen here). Will you be able to discover the correct number of coins and their precise locations?

Those squares containing numbers are empty, but where a number appears in a square, it indicates how many coins are located in the squares (up to a maximum of eight) surrounding the numbered one, touching it at any corner or side. There is only one coin in any individual square.

Place a circle into every square containing a coin.

0						2			0
		2		4		3	2		
0		3				2	2		
									1
	2		1		2			3	
			2				3		
1	2					0	2		
	3			3	2				1
	2	2							
			2			4		2	

Slitherlink

Draw a single continuous loop, by connecting the dots. No line may cross the path of another.

The figure inside each set of any four surrounding dots indicates the total number of surrounding lines.

Balancing the Scales

Given that scales A and B balance perfectly, how many diamonds are needed to balance scale C?

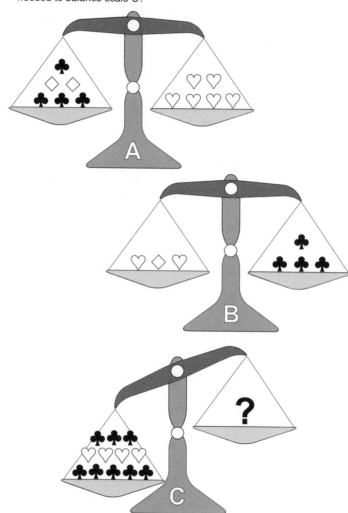

Every row and column of this grid should contain one each of the letters A, B, C, D, E and F. In addition, each of the six shapes (marked by thicker lines) should also contain one each of the letters A, B, C, D, E and F. Can you complete the grid?

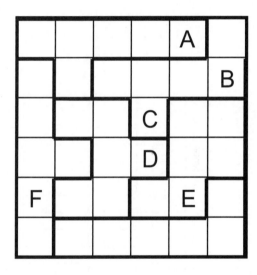

Piecework

Place all twelve of the pieces into the grid. Any may be rotated or flipped over, but none may touch another, not even diagonally. The numbers outside the grid refer to the number of consecutive black squares; and each block is separated from the others by at least one white square. For instance, '3 2' could refer to a row with none, one or more white squares, then three black squares, then at least one white square, then two more black squares, followed by any number of white squares.

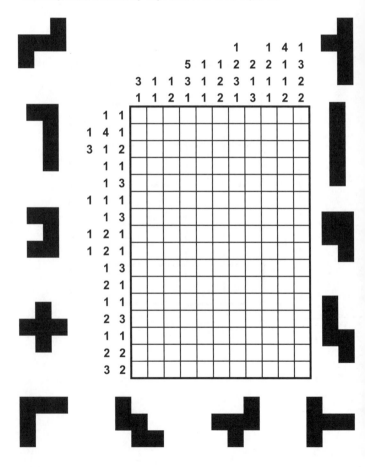

Tile Twister

Place the eight tiles into the puzzle grid so that all adjacent numbers on each tile match up. Tiles may be rotated through 360 degrees, but none may be flipped over.

4	1
3	3

4	1
1	2

3	1
1	2

2	1
3	2

		1	3		
		2	3		

1	4
3	4

1	3
4	1

2	1
3	4

2	3
3	1

Domino Placement

A standard set of twenty-eight dominoes has been laid out as shown. Can you draw in the edges of them all? The check-box is provided as an aid, so that you can see which dominoes have been located.

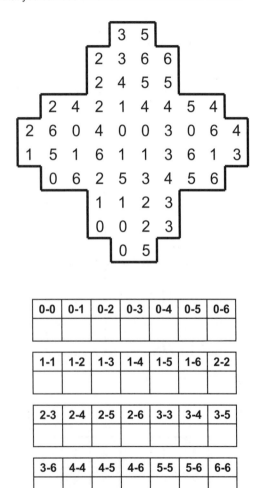

0-0	0-1	0-2	0-3	0-4	0-5	0-6

1-1	1-2	1-3	1-4	1-5	1-6	2-2

2-3	2-4	2-5	2-6	3-3	3-4	3-5

3-6	4-4	4-5	4-6	5-5	5-6	6-6

Hexagony

Can you place the hexagons into the grid, so that where any hexagon touches another along a straight line, the contents of both triangles is the same? No rotation of any hexagon is allowed!

Simple as A, B, C?

Each of the small squares in the grid below contains either A, B or C. Every row, column and each of the two long diagonals has exactly two of each letter. The information in the clues refers only to the squares in that row or column. To help you solve this problem, we have provided as many clues as we think you will need! Can you tell the letter in each square?

Across

1 The Cs are between the Bs.

2 The Cs are not in adjacent squares.

3 The Cs are further left than the Bs.

6 The Cs are further right than the As.

Down

1 Neither A is directly next to and below a C.

2 The Bs are lower than the Cs.

4 The Bs are higher than the As.

5 The As are higher than the Bs.

6 The As are between the Bs.

	1	2	3	4	5	6
1						
2						
3						
4						
5						
6						

Total Concentration

The blank squares below should be filled with whole numbers between 1 and 40 inclusive, any of which may occur more than once, or not at all.

The numbers in every horizontal row add up to the totals on the right, as do the two long diagonal lines; whilst those in every vertical column add up to the totals along the bottom.

Can you discover the missing numbers?

								161
	3	28	11		12	15	25	159
31	12		4	28	36		15	179
	15	18	40	13	34	27		152
33	35	31	2	12	26		13	168
31	19			39	22	8	39	219
37		5	23	18	11	10		167
	14		4	2		14	31	127
20	3	7			22	14	15	99
202	132	181	124	150	184	126	171	145

Shape Up

Every row and column in this grid originally contained one circle, one diamond, one square, one triangle and two blank squares, although not necessarily in that order.

Every symbol with a black arrow refers to the first of the four symbols encountered when travelling in the direction of the arrow. Every symbol with a white arrow refers to the second of the four symbols encountered in the direction of the arrow.

Can you complete the original grid?

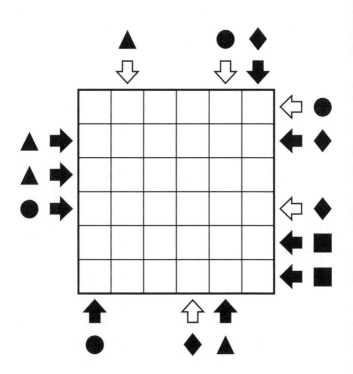

Given that the letters are valued 1-26 according to their places in the alphabet, can you crack the mystery code to reveal the missing letter?

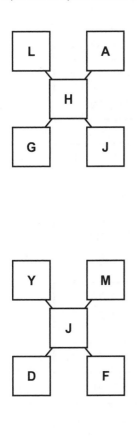

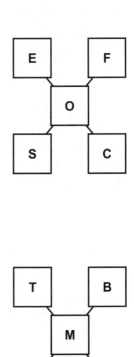

Whatever Next?

Which of the four lettered alternatives (A, B, C or D) fits most logically into
the empty square?

37	41	74
62	19	43
55	22	18

66	49	81
73	27	46
54	22	39

59	94	80
67	32	35
48	62	27

~~~~~~

66	41	56
73	21	54
34	19	47

A

52	73	61
97	24	63
47	39	38

B

38	54	94
58	17	41
77	37	21

C

85	69	71
96	37	49
35	41	58

D

Can you fill each square in the bottom line with the correct digit?

Every square in the solution contains only one digit from each of the lettered lines above, although two or more squares in the solution may contain the same digit.

At the end of every row is a score, which shows:

a   the number of digits placed in the correct finishing position on the bottom line, as indicated by a tick; and

b   the number of digits which appear on the bottom line, but in a different position, as indicated by a cross.

SCORE

A	1	2	3	4	✗
B	1	5	6	7	✗ ✗
C	5	6	4	3	✗ ✗
D	2	1	8	5	✗ ✗
E	3	1	2	7	✓ ✗
					✓ ✓ ✓ ✓

Combiku

Each horizontal row and vertical column should contain different shapes and different numbers.

Every square will contain one number and one shape and no combination may be repeated anywhere else in the puzzle; so, for instance, if a square contains a 3 and a star, then no other square containing a 3 will also contain a star and no other square with a star will contain a 3.

29

Ls in Place

Twelve L-shapes like the ones here need to be inserted in the grid and each L has one hole in it.

There are three pieces of each of the four kinds shown here and any piece may be turned or flipped over before being put in the grid. No pieces of the same kind touch, even at a corner.

The pieces fit together so well that you cannot see any spaces between them; only the holes show. Can you tell where the Ls are?

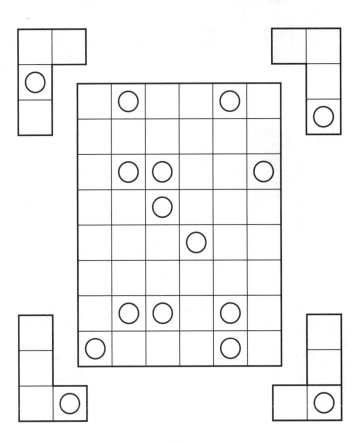

Box Clever

When the box below is folded to form a cube, just one of the five options (A, B, C, D or E) can be produced. Which?

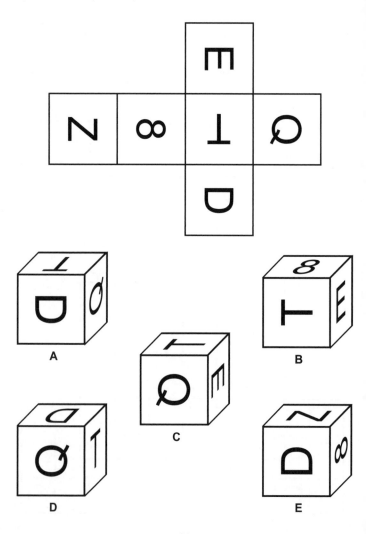

Latin Square

The grid should be filled with numbers from 1 to 6, so that each number appears just once in every row and column. The clues refer to the digit totals in the squares, eg A 1 2 3 = 6 means that the numbers in squares A1, A2 and A3 add up to 6.

1 C D 6 = 7
2 A 3 4 5 = 13
3 B 3 4 5 = 12
4 C 2 3 = 8
5 D 1 2 = 8
6 E 5 6 = 7
7 F 1 2 = 4
8 B C 1 = 9
9 A B 2 = 8
10 D E 3 = 9
11 E F 4 = 5

	A	B	C	D	E	F
1						
2						
3						
4						
5						
6						

Symbolism

Each of these squares should contain one or more symbols from the numbered square to the left of its particular horizontal row, plus one or more symbols from the lettered square above its particular vertical column. However, one square doesn't follow this rule. Which is the odd one out?

	A	B	C	D	E	F
	◄ ≈	♣ $	‡ ¿	♦ #	♪ ¶	Σ ☼
1 ∩ π	◄ ∩ / π	π / ∩ $	∩ / ¿ π	π / ∩#	♪ ∩ / π	☼ / π ∩
2 ♠ ß	♠ / ß ◄	ß / $ ♠	ß / ß ¿	#♠ / ♦	¶ ♪ / ♠ ß	Σ / ♠
3 £ ►	◄ / £ ≈	£ ♣ / ►	‡ / ► £	♦ ► / #	♪ / ►	£ Σ / ☼
4 Ω §	≈ / Ω	♣ Ω / $	‡ / §	♦ / §	¶ / Ω	Σ / Ω
5 Δ ♥	♥ / Δ ≈	♣ Δ / ♥ $	¿ / ♥	♥ / Δ ♦	♪ / Δ ♥	Σ Δ / ☼
6 ▲ ♫	≈ / ◄	▲ / ♣	‡ / ♫ ¿	# ♦ / ♫ ▲	¶ / ▲	Σ / ♫
7 ▼ φ	▼ / ≈ ◄	$ / ♣ φ	‡ / φ ▼	♦ / φ	¶ / ▼ ♪	▼ φ / ☼

Battleships

Can you place the vessels into the diagram? Some parts of vessels or sea squares have already been filled in. A number to the right or below a row or column refers to the number of occupied squares in that row or column.

Any vessel may be positioned horizontally or vertically, but no part of a vessel touches part of any other vessel, either horizontally, vertically or diagonally.

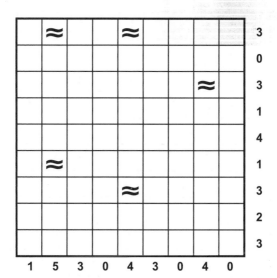

Empty Area of Sea: ≈

Aircraft Carrier: ◄■■►

Battleships: ◄■► ◄■►

Cruisers: ◄► ◄► ◄►

Submarines: ● ● ● ●

37

Coin Collecting

In this puzzle, an amateur coin collector has been out with his metal detector, searching for booty. He didn't have time to dig up all the coins he found, so has made a grid map, showing their locations, in the hope that if he loses the map, at least no-one else will understand it... However, he didn't count on YOU coming across the strange grid (as seen here). Will you be able to discover the correct number of coins and their precise locations?

Those squares containing numbers are empty, but where a number appears in a square, it indicates how many coins are located in the squares (up to a maximum of eight) surrounding the numbered one, touching it at any corner or side. There is only one coin in any individual square.

Place a circle into every square containing a coin.

		1	1		2		2		1
	3		3						
1					1		1	0	
	1	2							1
			3			1			
		2				0	1	1	
2			5			2			
	4					2			
			2		2		3	3	
2		3		0				0	

Draw a single continuous loop, by connecting the dots. No line may cross the path of another.

The figure inside each set of any four surrounding dots indicates the total number of surrounding lines.

Balancing the Scales

Given that scales A and B balance perfectly, how many clubs are needed to balance scale C?

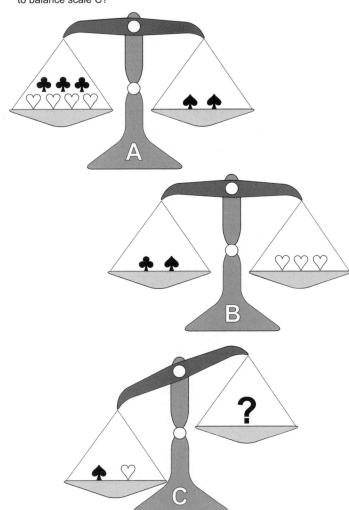

Logi-6

Every row and column of this grid should contain one each of the letters
A, B, C, D, E and F. In addition, each of the six shapes (marked by thicker
lines) should also contain one each of the letters A, B, C, D, E and F. Can
you complete the grid?

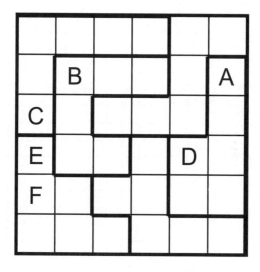

Piecework

Place all twelve of the pieces into the grid. Any may be rotated or flipped over, but none may touch another, not even diagonally. The numbers outside the grid refer to the number of consecutive black squares; and each block is separated from the others by at least one white square. For instance, '3 2' could refer to a row with none, one or more white squares, then three black squares, then at least one white square, then two more black squares, followed by any number of white squares.

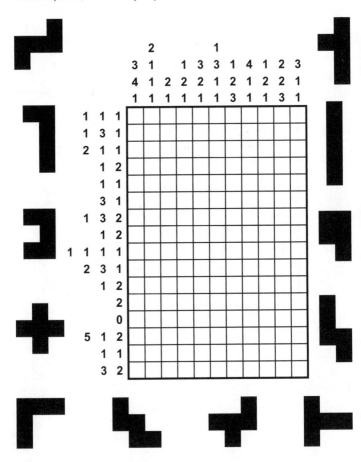

Tile Twister

Place the eight tiles into the puzzle grid so that all adjacent numbers on each tile match up. Tiles may be rotated through 360 degrees, but none may be flipped over.

1	2
3	1

4	1
2	4

4	1
1	2

1	1
1	1

				1	1
				4	3

4	2
4	1

3	1
2	4

2	4
1	1

3	3
4	2

43

Domino Placement

A standard set of twenty-eight dominoes has been laid out as shown.
Can you draw in the edges of them all? The check-box is provided as an
aid, so that you can see which dominoes have been located.

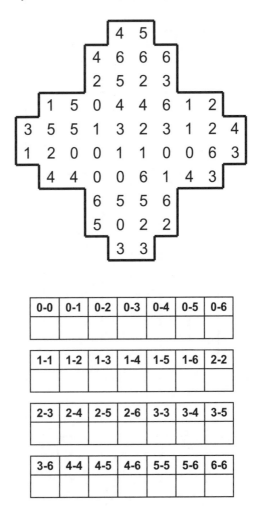

0-0	0-1	0-2	0-3	0-4	0-5	0-6

1-1	1-2	1-3	1-4	1-5	1-6	2-2

2-3	2-4	2-5	2-6	3-3	3-4	3-5

3-6	4-4	4-5	4-6	5-5	5-6	6-6

Can you place the hexagons into the grid, so that where any hexagon touches another along a straight line, the contents of both triangles is the same? No rotation of any hexagon is allowed!

Simple as A, B, C?

Each of the small squares in the grid below contains either A, B or C. Every row, column and each of the two long diagonals has exactly two of each letter. The information in the clues refers only to the squares in that row or column. To help you solve this problem, we have provided as many clues as we think you will need! Can you tell the letter in each square?

Across

1 The As are further right than the Bs.

2 The Bs are further left than the Cs.

4 The Cs are between the Bs.

5 The As are further left than the Cs.

6 Any three consecutive squares contain three different letters.

Down

2 The As are between the Bs.

4 The Bs are higher than the As.

6 Each A is directly next to and above a C.

	1	2	3	4	5	6
1						
2						
3						
4						
5						
6						

The blank squares below should be filled with whole numbers between 1 and 40 inclusive, any of which may occur more than once, or not at all.

The numbers in every horizontal row add up to the totals on the right, as do the two long diagonal lines; whilst those in every vertical column add up to the totals along the bottom.

Can you discover the missing numbers?

								155
10		22	14		8		10	124
	18	39	20	11				173
31	18		35	16	16	27	11	187
25	34	14	27	1		9	21	165
	9	10		34	19	8	22	114
15		38	37	9	24	10	3	149
22	20		4	36	13	19	40	187
24	36		32	38		9		188
162	161	217	176	178	135	135	123	171

45   Shape Up

Every row and column in this grid originally contained one circle, one diamond, one square, one triangle and two blank squares, although not necessarily in that order.

Every symbol with a black arrow refers to the first of the four symbols encountered when travelling in the direction of the arrow. Every symbol with a white arrow refers to the second of the four symbols encountered in the direction of the arrow.

Can you complete the original grid?

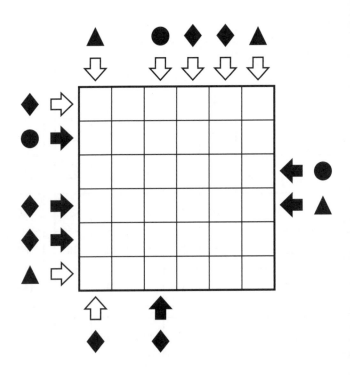

Given that the letters are valued 1-26 according to their places in the alphabet, can you crack the mystery code to reveal the missing letter?

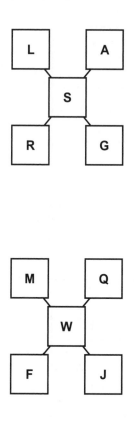

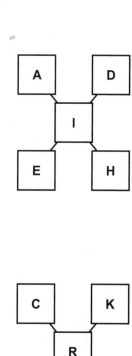

Whatever Next?

Which of the four lettered alternatives (A, B, C or D) fits most logically into the empty square?

3	9	5
8	17	4
6	3	8

4	5	4
6	13	2
3	3	7

2	4	6
8	12	3
2	7	3

6	2	5
3	13	7
4	8	1

A

4	4	8
5	16	2
7	2	6

B

5	2	3
3	10	1
2	4	4

C

6	3	1
2	11	4
3	2	6

D

The Bottom Line

Can you fill each square in the bottom line with the correct digit?

Every square in the solution contains only one digit from each of the lettered lines above, although two or more squares in the solution may contain the same digit.

At the end of every row is a score, which shows:

a the number of digits placed in the correct finishing position on the bottom line, as indicated by a tick; and

b the number of digits which appear on the bottom line, but in a different position, as indicated by a cross.

SCORE

A	1	2	3	4	✗
B	5	6	2	1	✗ ✗
C	7	3	4	8	✗ ✗
D	1	5	8	4	✓ ✗
E	2	8	3	6	✓ ✗
					✓ ✓ ✓ ✓

Combiku

Each horizontal row and vertical column should contain different shapes and different numbers.

Every square will contain one number and one shape and no combination may be repeated anywhere else in the puzzle; so, for instance, if a square contains a 3 and a star, then no other square containing a 3 will also contain a star and no other square with a star will contain a 3.

Twelve L-shapes like the ones here need to be inserted in the grid and each L has one hole in it.

There are three pieces of each of the four kinds shown here and any piece may be turned or flipped over before being put in the grid. No pieces of the same kind touch, even at a corner.

The pieces fit together so well that you cannot see any spaces between them; only the holes show. Can you tell where the Ls are?

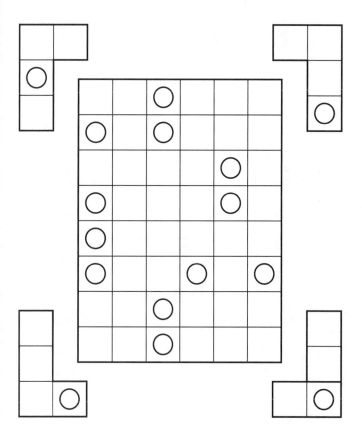

Box Clever

When the box below is folded to form a cube, just one of the five options (A, B, C, D or E) can be produced. Which?

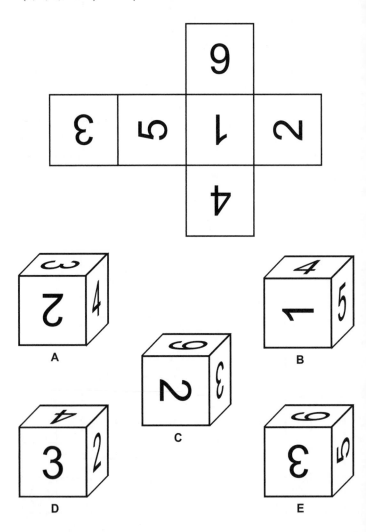

Latin Square

The grid should be filled with numbers from 1 to 6, so that each number appears just once in every row and column. The clues refer to the digit totals in the squares, eg A 1 2 3 = 6 means that the numbers in squares A1, A2 and A3 add up to 6.

1 B 4 5 = 6
2 C 2 3 = 8
3 D 1 2 = 3
4 E 4 5 6 = 10
5 F 5 6 = 6
6 E F 1 = 10
7 E F 2 = 8
8 D E 3 = 4
9 C D 4 = 11
10 C D 5 = 10
11 A B C 6 = 9

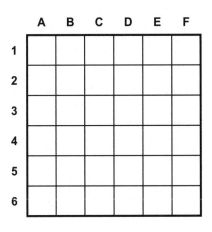

	A	B	C	D	E	F
1						
2						
3						
4						
5						
6						

Symbolism

Each of these squares should contain one or more symbols from the numbered square to the left of its particular horizontal row, plus one or more symbols from the lettered square above its particular vertical column. However, one square doesn't follow this rule. Which is the odd one out?

	A	B	C	D	E	F
	◄ ≈	♣ $	‡ ¿	♦ #	♪ ¶	Σ ☼
1	≈∩ / π	π / ∩♣	¿‡ / ∩	∩ / #♦	¶♪ / π	☼ / ∩
2	≈ / ♠◄	$♣ / ß	♠ / ¿ ß	♦ / ß	ß / ¶♠	♠Σ / ß
3	► / ◄≈	£ / $	► / ‡£	£# / ♦►	£♪ / ►	Σ / £
4	≈◄ / Ω	$ / §♣	‡¿ / Ω	# / §	Ω / ♪§	§ / Σ
5	♥ / ≈Δ	♣ / Δ	♥ / Δ	♥ / #	♪ / ♥Δ	Δ / Σ☼
6	▲ / ♫	▲ / $▲	¿ / ♫	▲♦ / ♫	♫ / ♪▲	♫ / ☼Σ
7	▼ / φ	◄ / ▼	‡φ / ▼	▼ / #	φ / ♪¶	☼ / ▼

Battleships

Can you place the vessels into the diagram? Some parts of vessels or sea squares have already been filled in. A number to the right or below a row or column refers to the number of occupied squares in that row or column.

Any vessel may be positioned horizontally or vertically, but no part of a vessel touches part of any other vessel, either horizontally, vertically or diagonally.

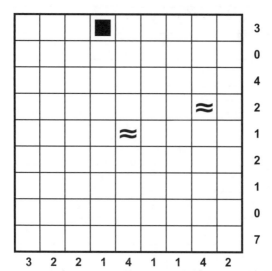

Empty Area of Sea: ≈

Aircraft Carrier: ◀■■▶

Battleships: ◀■▶ ◀■▶

Cruisers: ◀▶ ◀▶ ◀▶

Submarines: ● ● ● ●

			■						3
									0
									4
							≈		2
				≈					1
									2
									1
									0
									7
3	2	2	1	4	1	1	4	2	

Coin Collecting

In this puzzle, an amateur coin collector has been out with his metal detector, searching for booty. He didn't have time to dig up all the coins he found, so has made a grid map, showing their locations, in the hope that if he loses the map, at least no-one else will understand it... However, he didn't count on YOU coming across the strange grid (as seen here). Will you be able to discover the correct number of coins and their precise locations?

Those squares containing numbers are empty, but where a number appears in a square, it indicates how many coins are located in the squares (up to a maximum of eight) surrounding the numbered one, touching it at any corner or side. There is only one coin in any individual square.

Place a circle into every square containing a coin.

	3		3	2	1				1
								2	
		1			5			3	3
	0	0							
		1			2		1		
2			1					1	
					0	1			
4				2			3		2
		3							2
3			2		1			2	

Draw a single continuous loop, by connecting the dots. No line may cross the path of another.

The figure inside each set of any four surrounding dots indicates the total number of surrounding lines.

```
.   .   .   .   .   .   .   .   .   .   .
        3       3       3   1
.   .   .   .   .   .   .   .   .   .   .
  1   0       1   2   2           1
.   .   .   .   .   .   .   .   .   .   .
  1               2       1   3   2
.   .   .   .   .   .   .   .   .   .   .
            3   1   2   2       1
.   .   .   .   .   .   .   .   .   .   .
  1               2       2       1   2
.   .   .   .   .   .   .   .   .   .   .
      0       3       3   2   2
.   .   .   .   .   .   .   .   .   .   .
      3               1   1           2
.   .   .   .   .   .   .   .   .   .   .
                  2   1   1       2
.   .   .   .   .   .   .   .   .   .   .
      3       3   2   2       1
.   .   .   .   .   .   .   .   .   .   .
      0   2       1           0
.   .   .   .   .   .   .   .   .   .   .
      1                       3   2
.   .   .   .   .   .   .   .   .   .   .
      3       2   1       1   2
.   .   .   .   .   .   .   .   .   .   .
```

Balancing the Scales

Given that scales A and B balance perfectly, how many spades are needed to balance scale C?

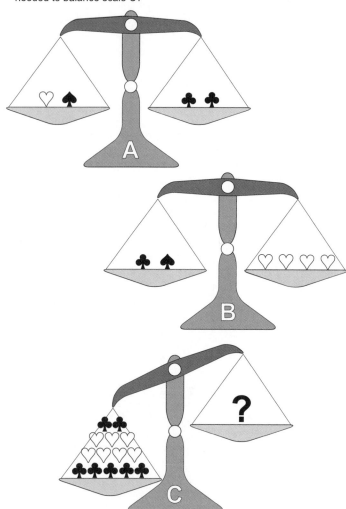

Logi-6

Every row and column of this grid should contain one each of the letters A, B, C, D, E and F. In addition, each of the six shapes (marked by thicker lines) should also contain one each of the letters A, B, C, D, E and F. Can you complete the grid?

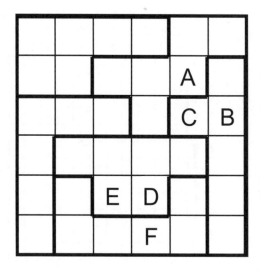

Piecework

Place all twelve of the pieces into the grid. Any may be rotated or flipped over, but none may touch another, not even diagonally. The numbers outside the grid refer to the number of consecutive black squares; and each block is separated from the others by at least one white square. For instance, '3 2' could refer to a row with none, one or more white squares, then three black squares, then at least one white square, then two more black squares, followed by any number of white squares.

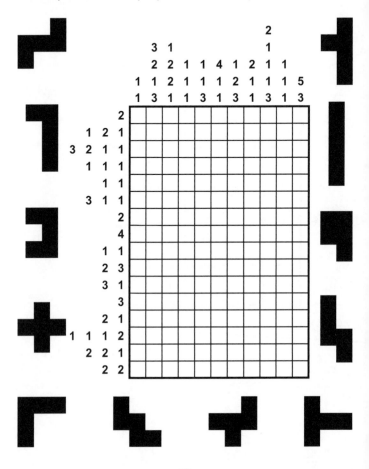

Tile Twister

Place the eight tiles into the puzzle grid so that all adjacent numbers on each tile match up. Tiles may be rotated through 360 degrees, but none may be flipped over.

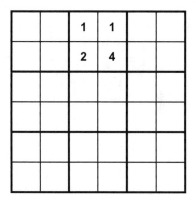

Domino Placement

A standard set of twenty-eight dominoes has been laid out as shown. Can you draw in the edges of them all? The check-box is provided as an aid, so that you can see which dominoes have been located.

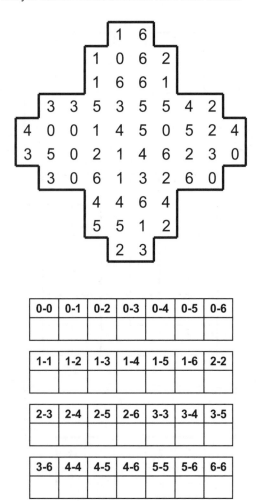

0-0	0-1	0-2	0-3	0-4	0-5	0-6

1-1	1-2	1-3	1-4	1-5	1-6	2-2

2-3	2-4	2-5	2-6	3-3	3-4	3-5

3-6	4-4	4-5	4-6	5-5	5-6	6-6

Hexagony

62

Can you place the hexagons into the grid, so that where any hexagon touches another along a straight line, the contents of both triangles is the same? No rotation of any hexagon is allowed!

Simple as A, B, C?

Each of the small squares in the grid below contains either A, B or C. Every row, column and each of the two long diagonals has exactly two of each letter. The information in the clues refers only to the squares in that row or column. To help you solve this problem, we have provided as many clues as we think you will need! Can you tell the letter in each square?

Across

1 The two Bs are separated by one square, which contains a C.

5 The Bs are between the Cs.

6 The Cs are between the As.

Down

1 The Bs are lower than the As.

2 The Cs are between the As.

3 Each B is directly next to and below an A.

4 Each C is directly next to and below an A.

5 The Bs are between the Cs.

6 The As are between the Bs.

	1	2	3	4	5	6
1						
2						
3						
4						
5						
6						

Total Concentration

64

The blank squares below should be filled with whole numbers between 1 and 40 inclusive, any of which may occur more than once, or not at all.

The numbers in every horizontal row add up to the totals on the right, as do the two long diagonal lines; whilst those in every vertical column add up to the totals along the bottom.

Can you discover the missing numbers?

								172

22	9	40	37	37		34	7	195
39	2	31	18			36	8	207
38	39	8	8		30	30	19	174
	22	10		7	7		16	158
24		1	38	38		27		173
	31		9	12	21	40		160
		16	27	25	39	2	18	171
38	7	35		12		20	31	175
232	153	143	172	169	173	223	148	151

67

Shape Up

Every row and column in this grid originally contained one circle, one diamond, one square, one triangle and two blank squares, although not necessarily in that order.

Every symbol with a black arrow refers to the first of the four symbols encountered when travelling in the direction of the arrow. Every symbol with a white arrow refers to the second of the four symbols encountered in the direction of the arrow.

Can you complete the original grid?

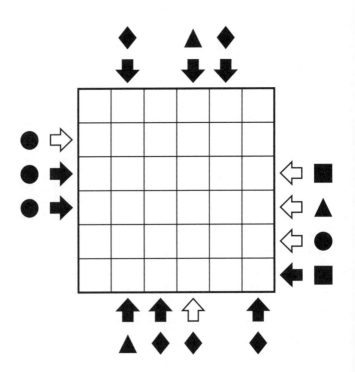

Given that the letters are valued 1-26 according to their places in the alphabet, can you crack the mystery code to reveal the missing letter?

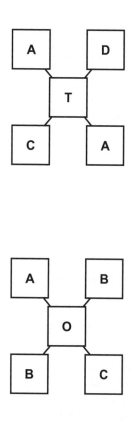

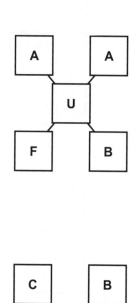

Whatever Next?

Which of the four lettered alternatives (A, B, C or D) fits most logically into the empty square?

16	15	18
10	11	13
21	19	17

21	17	22
13	13	11
19	20	18

26	19	14
7	16	20
13	24	21

?

17	19	21
16	15	17
15	9	18

A

14	17	23
18	19	19
16	10	22

B

22	16	19
20	14	8
18	26	19

C

16	15	28
7	26	13
20	17	19

D

The Bottom Line

Can you fill each square in the bottom line with the correct digit?

Every square in the solution contains only one digit from each of the lettered lines above, although two or more squares in the solution may contain the same digit.

At the end of every row is a score, which shows:

- **a** the number of digits placed in the correct finishing position on the bottom line, as indicated by a tick; and

- **b** the number of digits which appear on the bottom line, but in a different position, as indicated by a cross.

SCORE

A	1	2	3	4	✗
B	5	6	2	7	✗
C	4	8	7	8	✗ ✗
D	8	3	4	5	✗ ✗
E	3	4	8	6	✓ ✗
					✓✓✓✓

Combiku

Each horizontal row and vertical column should contain different shapes and different numbers.

Every square will contain one number and one shape and no combination may be repeated anywhere else in the puzzle; so, for instance, if a square contains a 3 and a star, then no other square containing a 3 will also contain a star and no other square with a star will contain a 3.

Ls in Place

Twelve L-shapes like the ones here need to be inserted in the grid and each L has one hole in it.

There are three pieces of each of the four kinds shown here and any piece may be turned or flipped over before being put in the grid. No pieces of the same kind touch, even at a corner.

The pieces fit together so well that you cannot see any spaces between them; only the holes show. Can you tell where the Ls are?

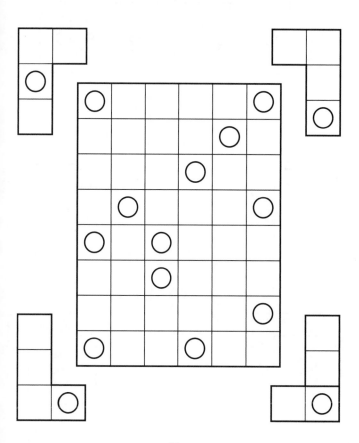

Box Clever

When the box below is folded to form a cube, just one of the five options (A, B, C, D or E) can be produced. Which?

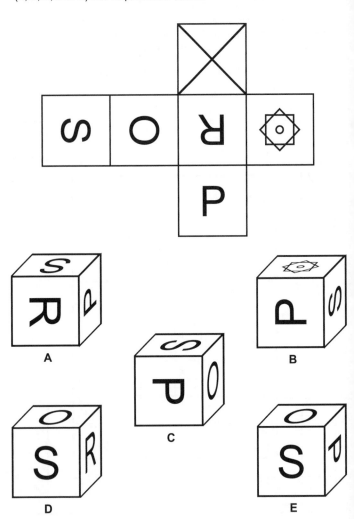

A

B

C

D

E

Latin Square

The grid should be filled with numbers from 1 to 6, so that each number appears just once in every row and column. The clues refer to the digit totals in the squares, eg A 1 2 3 = 6 means that the numbers in squares A1, A2 and A3 add up to 6.

1. E 1 2 = 9
2. F 2 3 4 = 6
3. A B 1 = 8
4. A B C 2 = 10
5. A B 3 = 10
6. A B 4 = 8
7. C D 5 = 11
8. E F 6 = 10
9. A 5 6 = 7
10. B 5 6 = 4
11. C 3 4 = 7

	A	B	C	D	E	F
1						
2						
3						
4						
5						
6						

Symbolism

Each of these squares should contain one or more symbols from the numbered square to the left of its particular horizontal row, plus one or more symbols from the lettered square above its particular vertical column. However, one square doesn't follow this rule. Which is the odd one out?

	A	B	C	D	E	F
	◄ ≈	♣ $	‡ ¿	♦ #	♪ ¶	Σ ☼
1 ∩ π	∩ ≈ / ◄	♣ / π ∩	‡ / ¿ π	# / ∩ ♦	∩ π / ¶	☼ / π
2 ♠ ß	≈ ß / ◄	♣ / $ ♠	‡ / ♠ ¿	# / ß ♠	♠ ß / ♪	ß / Σ ♠
3 £ ►	► / ≈ ◄	♣ / £	£ / ¿	♦ ► / #	£ ► / ¶	☼ / ►
4 Ω §	≈ § / ◄	♣ / § Ω	§ / ‡	Ω § / ♦	¶ / Ω	Ω / Σ
5 Δ ♥	Δ ♥ / ≈	Δ / ♣	¿ ‡ / ♥	# ♦ / ♥	♪ / ♥	Δ Σ / ☼
6 ▲ ♫	▲ ♫ / ≈	$ / ♣	‡ / ♫ ▲	# / ▲	♫ / ♪	▲ / Σ
7 ▼ φ	◄ / ▼	♣ / φ ▼	φ / ‡	▼ ♦ / #	φ / ¶	▼ / ☼

Battleships

Can you place the vessels into the diagram? Some parts of vessels or sea squares have already been filled in. A number to the right or below a row or column refers to the number of occupied squares in that row or column.

Any vessel may be positioned horizontally or vertically, but no part of a vessel touches part of any other vessel, either horizontally, vertically or diagonally.

Empty Area of Sea: ≈

Aircraft Carrier: ◄■ ■►

Battleships: ◄■► ◄■►

Cruisers: ◄► ◄► ◄►

Submarines: ● ● ● ●

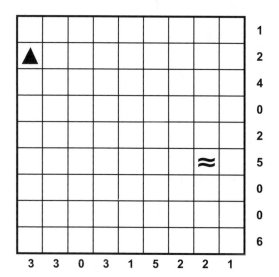

Coin Collecting

In this puzzle, an amateur coin collector has been out with his metal detector, searching for booty. He didn't have time to dig up all the coins he found, so has made a grid map, showing their locations, in the hope that if he loses the map, at least no-one else will understand it... However, he didn't count on YOU coming across the strange grid (as seen here). Will you be able to discover the correct number of coins and their precise locations?

Those squares containing numbers are empty, but where a number appears in a square, it indicates how many coins are located in the squares (up to a maximum of eight) surrounding the numbered one, touching it at any corner or side. There is only one coin in any individual square.

Place a circle into every square containing a coin.

		0			0				
0							1		0
		2		1	0				
	3								
				3		2	2		
	5		3		1				
	2		1						4
	5								
			1	3			4	4	
	3					2			

Draw a single continuous loop, by connecting the dots. No line may cross the path of another.

The figure inside each set of any four surrounding dots indicates the total number of surrounding lines.

```
.   .   .   .   .   .   .   .   .   .   .
        2   3       0       0
.   .   .   .   .   .   .   .   .   .   .
                    3       1   2   3
.   .   .   .   .   .   .   .   .   .   .
    2   1       0           2   2
.   .   .   .   .   .   .   .   .   .   .
    3   1                       1
.   .   .   .   .   .   .   .   .   .   .
        1       0       0
.   .   .   .   .   .   .   .   .   .   .
    2           1       2           0
.   .   .   .   .   .   .   .   .   .   .
  3 2   1           1       1   1
.   .   .   .   .   .   .   .   .   .   .
    1       0   1       3
.   .   .   .   .   .   .   .   .   .   .
  0 1   3       0   1       1
.   .   .   .   .   .   .   .   .   .   .
  2     2   1   1   1   0       1   2
.   .   .   .   .   .   .   .   .   .   .
    1           2       1
.   .   .   .   .   .   .   .   .   .   .
    2           2           1   2   3
.   .   .   .   .   .   .   .   .   .   .
```

Balancing the Scales

Given that scales A and B balance perfectly, how many diamonds are needed to balance scale C?

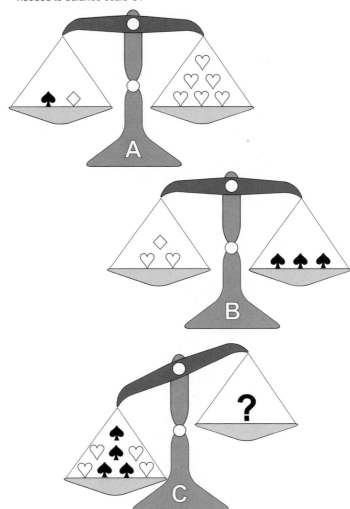

Logi-6

Every row and column of this grid should contain one each of the letters A, B, C, D, E and F. In addition, each of the six shapes (marked by thicker lines) should also contain one each of the letters A, B, C, D, E and F. Can you complete the grid?

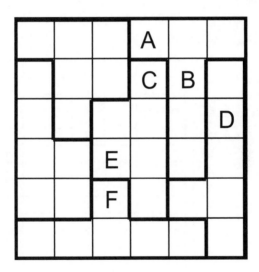

Piecework

Place all twelve of the pieces into the grid. Any may be rotated or flipped over, but none may touch another, not even diagonally. The numbers outside the grid refer to the number of consecutive black squares; and each block is separated from the others by at least one white square. For instance, '3 2' could refer to a row with none, one or more white squares, then three black squares, then at least one white square, then two more black squares, followed by any number of white squares.

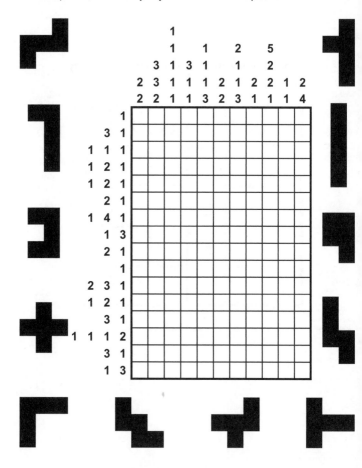

Tile Twister

Place the eight tiles into the puzzle grid so that all adjacent numbers on each tile match up. Tiles may be rotated through 360 degrees, but none may be flipped over.

1	2
3	4

3	2
2	3

3	3
4	2

1	3
2	4

1	3				
3	2				

1	4
1	2

4	1
3	2

3	1
3	4

1	1
2	3

Domino Placement

A standard set of twenty-eight dominoes has been laid out as shown.
Can you draw in the edges of them all? The check-box is provided as an
aid, so that you can see which dominoes have been located.

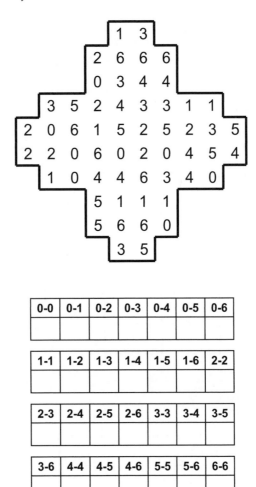

	1 3	

```
        1  3
     2  6  6  6
     0  3  4  4
  3  5  2  4  3  3  1  1
2  0  6  1  5  2  5  2  3  5
2  2  0  6  0  2  0  4  5  4
  1  0  4  4  6  3  4  0
     5  1  1  1
     5  6  6  0
        3  5
```

0-0	0-1	0-2	0-3	0-4	0-5	0-6

1-1	1-2	1-3	1-4	1-5	1-6	2-2

2-3	2-4	2-5	2-6	3-3	3-4	3-5

3-6	4-4	4-5	4-6	5-5	5-6	6-6

Hexagony

Can you place the hexagons into the grid, so that where any hexagon touches another along a straight line, the contents of both triangles is the same? No rotation of any hexagon is allowed!

Simple as A, B, C?

Each of the small squares in the grid below contains either A, B or C. Every row, column and each of the two long diagonals has exactly two of each letter. The information in the clues refers only to the squares in that row or column. To help you solve this problem, we have provided as many clues as we think you will need! Can you tell the letter in each square?

Across

1 The As are between the Bs.

4 The Bs are between the Cs.

5 Each A is directly next to and left of a C.

6 The Bs are between the As.

Down

1 Each A is directly next to and above a B.

5 The As are between the Bs.

6 The As are lower than the Cs.

	1	2	3	4	5	6
1						
2						
3						
4						
5						
6						

Total Concentration

The blank squares below should be filled with whole numbers between 1 and 40 inclusive, any of which may occur more than once, or not at all.

The numbers in every horizontal row add up to the totals on the right, as do the two long diagonal lines; whilst those in every vertical column add up to the totals along the bottom.

Can you discover the missing numbers?

								234
9	15	26	18	4		9	26	125
	34	23	12	19	9		35	196
27		25	24	39	39	17		212
14	36		12	34	29		13	189
15	2	3			38		6	125
30	7	34			18	7	34	167
		12	23	24		18		104
37	33	38	12	20		7	35	186
170	163	174	145	191	166	129	166	178

Shape Up

Every row and column in this grid originally contained one circle, one diamond, one square, one triangle and two blank squares, although not necessarily in that order.

Every symbol with a black arrow refers to the first of the four symbols encountered when travelling in the direction of the arrow. Every symbol with a white arrow refers to the second of the four symbols encountered in the direction of the arrow.

Can you complete the original grid?

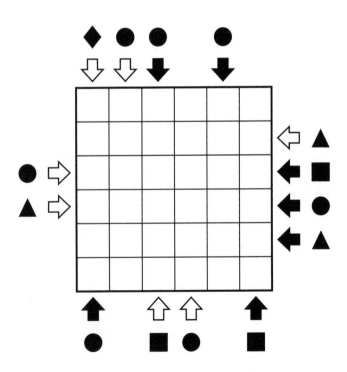

Given that the letters are valued 1-26 according to their places in the alphabet, can you crack the mystery code to reveal the missing letter?

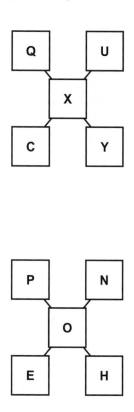

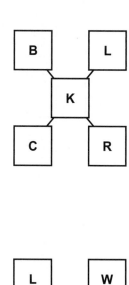

Whatever Next?

Which of the four lettered alternatives (A, B, C or D) fits most logically into the empty square?

S	G	K
A	19	E
M	W	Q

M	Q	E
C	13	K
A	G	S

E	G	Q
K	31	W
S	C	A

A	M	W
C	11	Q
G	E	S

A

S	A	W
E	27	C
M	Q	G

B

A	M	G
E	15	S
Q	H	C

C

G	K	W
I	23	C
A	E	H

D

The Bottom Line

Can you fill each square in the bottom line with the correct digit?

Every square in the solution contains only one digit from each of the lettered lines above, although two or more squares in the solution may contain the same digit.

At the end of every row is a score, which shows:

a   the number of digits placed in the correct finishing
    position on the bottom line, as indicated by a tick; and

b   the number of digits which appear on the bottom line,
    but in a different position, as indicated by a cross.

SCORE

A	1	2	3	4	✗
B	4	1	1	5	✗
C	2	3	6	6	✗
D	5	7	8	8	✗
E	7	4	7	3	✓
					✓✓✓✓

Combiku

Each horizontal row and vertical column should contain different shapes and different numbers.

Every square will contain one number and one shape and no combination may be repeated anywhere else in the puzzle; so, for instance, if a square contains a 3 and a star, then no other square containing a 3 will also contain a star and no other square with a star will contain a 3.

Ls in Place

Twelve L-shapes like the ones here need to be inserted in the grid and each L has one hole in it.

There are three pieces of each of the four kinds shown here and any piece may be turned or flipped over before being put in the grid. No pieces of the same kind touch, even at a corner.

The pieces fit together so well that you cannot see any spaces between them; only the holes show. Can you tell where the Ls are?

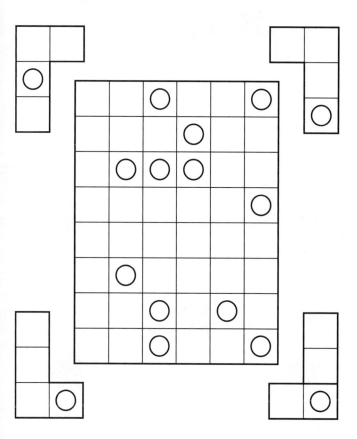

Box Clever

When the box below is folded to form a cube, just one of the five options
(A, B, C, D or E) can be produced. Which?

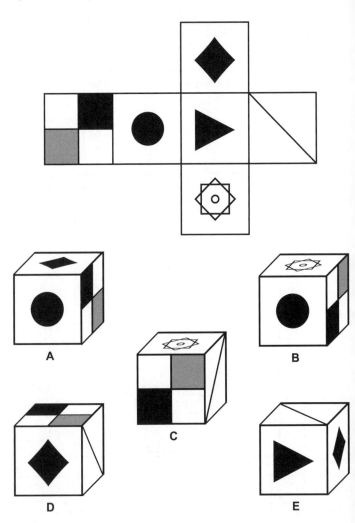

A

B

C

D

E

Latin Square

The grid should be filled with numbers from 1 to 6, so that each number appears just once in every row and column. The clues refer to the digit totals in the squares, eg A 1 2 3 = 6 means that the numbers in squares A1, A2 and A3 add up to 6.

1 D E F 5 = 10
2 A B C 6 = 12
3 A 3 4 = 4
4 B 1 2 = 11
5 C 4 5 = 10
6 D 1 2 = 7
7 E 3 4 = 8
8 F 3 4 = 7
9 E F 1 = 4
10 E F 2 = 7
11 C D 3 = 11

	A	B	C	D	E	F
1						
2						
3						
4						
5						
6						

Symbolism

Each of these squares should contain one or more symbols from the numbered square to the left of its particular horizontal row, plus one or more symbols from the lettered square above its particular vertical column. However, one square doesn't follow this rule. Which is the odd one out?

	A	B	C	D	E	F
	◄ ≈	♣ $	‡ ¿	♦ #	♪ ¶	Σ ☼
1 ∩ π	π ∩ ≈	$ ∩	‡ π ¿	∩ π ♦	¶ π ♪	☼ Σ ∩
2 ♠ ß	♠ ◄	♣ ß ♠	ß ¿	♦ ♠ #	¶ ♪ ß	♠ ☼
3 £ ▶	£ ≈	$ £	▶ ‡	# ▶ ♦	▶ £ ¶	▶ Σ £
4 Ω §	◄ Ω ≈	§ ♣	¿ Ω ‡	♦ Ω §	§ ♪	☼ Ω
5 Δ ♥	◄ ♥ Δ	♥ $	Δ ¿	♥ #	♪ ♥	Δ ☼
6 ▲ ♫	≈ ▲ ♫	▲ $	‡ ♫	# ▲	♫ ¶	♫ ▲ ☼
7 ▼ φ	◄ φ	▼ $ ♣	φ ‡	φ ♦	▼ ♪	Σ ☼

Battleships

Can you place the vessels into the diagram? Some parts of vessels or sea squares have already been filled in. A number to the right or below a row or column refers to the number of occupied squares in that row or column.

Any vessel may be positioned horizontally or vertically, but no part of a vessel touches part of any other vessel, either horizontally, vertically or diagonally.

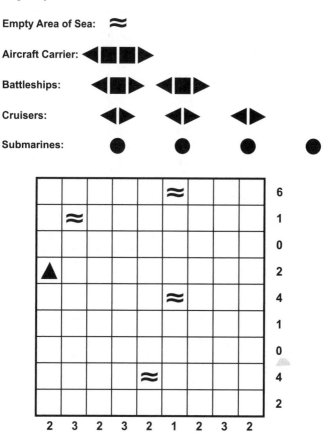

Empty Area of Sea:

Aircraft Carrier:

Battleships:

Cruisers:

Submarines:

6
1
0
2
4
1
0
4
2

2 3 2 3 2 1 2 3 2

Coin Collecting

In this puzzle, an amateur coin collector has been out with his metal detector, searching for booty. He didn't have time to dig up all the coins he found, so has made a grid map, showing their locations, in the hope that if he loses the map, at least no-one else will understand it... However, he didn't count on YOU coming across the strange grid (as seen here). Will you be able to discover the correct number of coins and their precise locations?

Those squares containing numbers are empty, but where a number appears in a square, it indicates how many coins are located in the squares (up to a maximum of eight) surrounding the numbered one, touching it at any corner or side. There is only one coin in any individual square.

Place a circle into every square containing a coin.

	3					1			
			4	2	1		1	2	
	2		2		1	1			2
1						2	2	3	
				3					
1		3			3	1		2	2
		1	2				2		1
		1						1	
4		3			1				1
			0			1			

Slitherlink

Draw a single continuous loop, by connecting the dots. No line may cross the path of another.

The figure inside each set of any four surrounding dots indicates the total number of surrounding lines.

```
.   .   .   .   .   .   .   .   .   .   .   .
      1   1   2       3
.   .   .   .   .   .   .   .   .   .   .   .
      0       2           1   2
.   .   .   .   .   .   .   .   .   .   .   .
      1   3   2   2   1       2
.   .   .   .   .   .   .   .   .   .   .   .
      0   1   1   1           3   1
.   .   .   .   .   .   .   .   .   .   .   .
  1                   1
.   .   .   .   .   .   .   .   .   .   .   .
                      3                   0
.   .   .   .   .   .   .   .   .   .   .   .
      1   0   0           3   1
.   .   .   .   .   .   .   .   .   .   .   .
      3           3   1           2
.   .   .   .   .   .   .   .   .   .   .   .
      2   0           2       3   1
.   .   .   .   .   .   .   .   .   .   .   .
  1   3               3           3   2
.   .   .   .   .   .   .   .   .   .   .   .
          1   0       3   2
.   .   .   .   .   .   .   .   .   .   .   .
  3               1           1   2
.   .   .   .   .   .   .   .   .   .   .   .
```

Balancing the Scales

Given that scales A and B balance perfectly, how many hearts are needed to balance scale C?

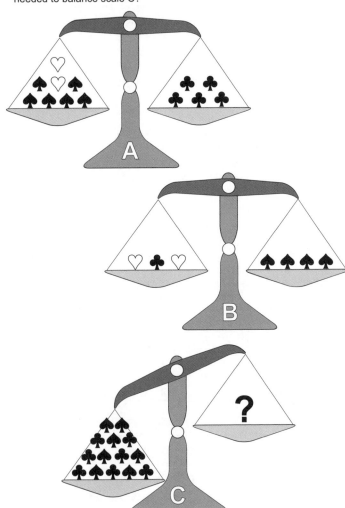

Logi-6

Every row and column of this grid should contain one each of the letters
A, B, C, D, E and F. In addition, each of the six shapes (marked by thicker
lines) should also contain one each of the letters A, B, C, D, E and F. Can
you complete the grid?

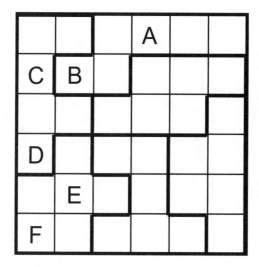

Piecework

Place all twelve of the pieces into the grid. Any may be rotated or flipped over, but none may touch another, not even diagonally. The numbers outside the grid refer to the number of consecutive black squares; and each block is separated from the others by at least one white square. For instance, '3 2' could refer to a row with none, one or more white squares, then three black squares, then at least one white square, then two more black squares, followed by any number of white squares.

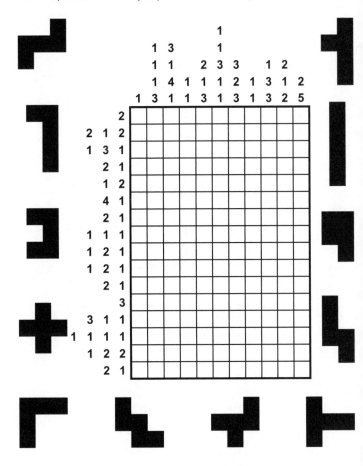

Tile Twister

Place the eight tiles into the puzzle grid so that all adjacent numbers on each tile match up. Tiles may be rotated through 360 degrees, but none may be flipped over.

2	3
4	4

2	4
2	2

2	1
2	2

3	3
4	2

				2	1
				3	1

2	1
4	4

3	2
1	4

3	1
2	2

2	3
1	3

Solutions

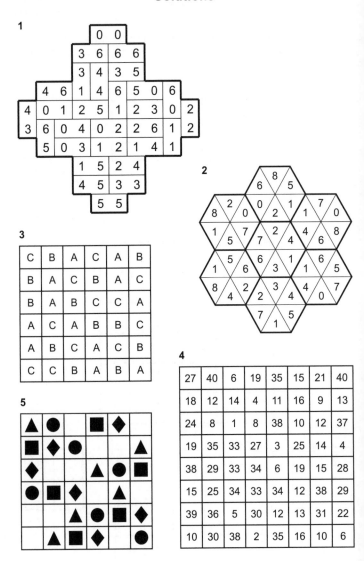

1

	0	0	

| 3 | 6 | 6 | 6 |
| 3 | 4 | 3 | 5 |

4	6	1	4	6	5	0	6
4	0	1	2	5	1	2	3	0	2
3	6	0	4	0	2	2	6	1	2
	5	0	3	1	2	1	4	1

1	5	2	4
4	5	3	3
	5	5	

2

3

C	B	A	C	A	B
B	A	C	B	A	C
B	A	B	C	C	A
A	C	A	B	B	C
A	B	C	A	C	B
C	C	B	A	B	A

5

4

27	40	6	19	35	15	21	40
18	12	14	4	11	16	9	13
24	8	1	8	38	10	12	37
19	35	33	27	3	25	14	4
38	29	33	34	6	19	15	28
15	25	34	33	34	12	38	29
39	36	5	30	12	13	31	22
10	30	38	2	35	16	10	6

Solutions

6

The value of the central letter is the total value of the two letters in the highest boxes and also the total value of the two letters in the lowest boxes. Thus the missing value is 18, so the missing letter is R.

7

D – All are square or cube numbers.

8

6814

9

Solutions

10

11
C

12

5	6	4	3	1	2
2	1	5	4	6	3
6	2	3	5	4	1
4	5	1	2	3	6
1	3	2	6	5	4
3	4	6	1	2	5

13
E4

14

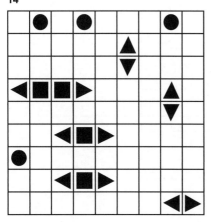

Solutions

15

0					●	2	●		0
		2	●	4		3	2		
0		3	●		●	2	2	●	
		●				●			1
●	2		1		2	●	●	3	
			2				3	●	●
1	2	●		●		0	2		
●	3		●	3	2			●	1
●	2	2	●			●	●		
			2	●	●	4	●	2	

16

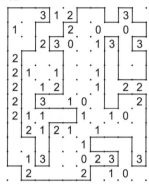

17

8 – Since 4 clubs = 1 diamond + 2 hearts (scale B), replace the 4 clubs in scale A with 1 diamond and 2 hearts, so that 3 diamonds + 2 hearts = 6 hearts. Thus 3 diamonds = 4 hearts. Multiply the quantities in scale B by two, so that 2 diamonds + 4 hearts = 8 clubs. Now replace these 4 hearts with 3 diamonds, so that 5 diamonds = 8 clubs. In scale C there are 4 hearts (the same as 3 diamonds, above) and 8 clubs (the same as 5 diamonds, above). So 8 diamonds are needed to balance scale C.

Solutions

18

B	D	C	F	A	E
C	E	D	A	F	B
E	F	B	C	D	A
A	B	E	D	C	F
F	C	A	B	E	D
D	A	F	E	B	C

19

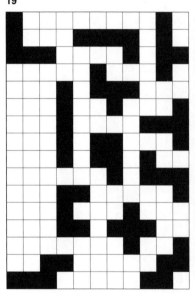

20

3	2	2	1	1	4
4	1	1	3	3	4
4	1	1	3	3	4
1	2	2	3	3	1
1	2	2	3	3	1
2	3	3	1	1	4

Solutions

21

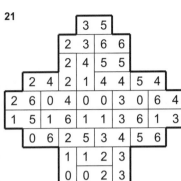

		3	5						
	2	3	6	6					
	2	4	5	5					
2	4	2	1	4	4	5	4		
2	6	0	4	0	0	3	0	6	4
1	5	1	6	1	1	3	6	1	3
	0	6	2	5	3	4	5	6	
		1	1	2	3				
		0	0	2	3				
			0	5					

22

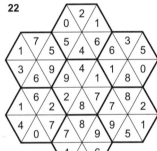

23

A	A	B	C	C	B
B	C	A	B	C	A
C	C	B	B	A	A
C	B	C	A	A	B
B	A	C	A	B	C
A	B	A	C	B	C

24

34	3	28	11	31	12	15	25
31	12	31	4	28	36	22	15
4	15	18	40	13	34	27	1
33	35	31	2	12	26	16	13
31	19	32	29	39	22	8	39
37	31	5	23	18	11	10	32
12	14	29	4	2	21	14	31
20	3	7	11	7	22	14	15

25

■		▲	●	◆	
▲	■			●	◆
	▲	◆	■		●
	●	■	◆		▲
◆		●	▲	■	
●	◆			▲	■

Solutions

26

The value of the central letter is the total value of the two letters in the furthest left boxes minus the total value of the two letters in the furthest right boxes. Thus the missing value is 16, so the missing letter is P.

27

C – The number in each top corner has the centre square number subtracted from it to equal the number in the opposite corner; likewise the top row middle number and its opposite and the left column middle number and its opposite.

28

3758

29

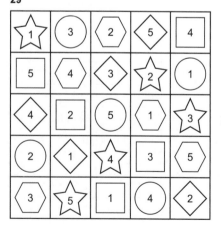

Solutions

30

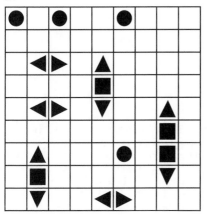

31
D

32

2	4	5	6	1	3
5	3	6	2	4	1
4	1	2	3	6	5
6	5	4	1	3	2
3	6	1	5	2	4
1	2	3	4	5	6

33
A6

34

Solutions

35

	●	1	1	●	2	●	2	●	1
●	3		3						
1		●	●		1		1	0	
	1	2				●			1
			3	●		1		●	
●		2	●	●		0	1	1	
2		●	5	●		2			
●	4		●		●	2	●	●	●
	●	●	2		2		3	3	
2	●	3		0		●		0	

36

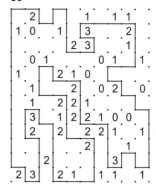

37

9 – Multiply the quantities in scale B by two, so that 2 spades + 2 clubs = 6 hearts. Now replace those 2 spades with their value in scale A, so that 3 clubs + 4 hearts + 2 clubs = 6 hearts. Thus 5 clubs = 2 hearts. Replace the 4 hearts in scale A with 10 clubs. Thus 3 clubs + 10 clubs = 2 spades, so 13 clubs = 2 spades. Since 2 spades = 13 clubs and 2 hearts = 5 clubs (above), 2 spades + 2 hearts = 18 clubs. There is 1 spade and 1 heart in scale C. Thus a total of 9 clubs are needed to balance scale C.

Solutions

38

A	E	F	B	C	D
D	B	C	E	F	A
C	D	E	A	B	F
E	F	A	C	D	B
F	A	B	D	E	C
B	C	D	F	A	E

39

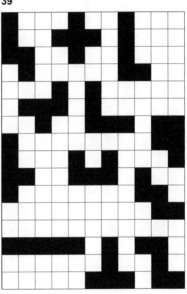

40

4	4	4	1	1	1
1	2	2	1	1	1
1	2	2	1	1	1
3	1	1	4	4	3
3	1	1	4	4	3
2	4	4	2	2	3

41

```
      4 5
    4 6 6 6
    2 5 2 3
1 5 0 4 4 6 1 2
3 5 5 1 3 2 3 1 2 4
1 2 0 0 1 1 0 0 6 3
  4 4 0 0 6 1 4 3
      6 5 5 6
      5 0 2 2
      3 3
```

42

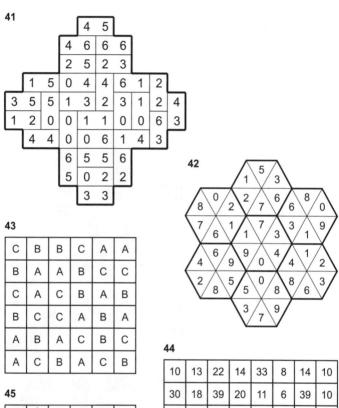

43

C	B	B	C	A	A
B	A	A	B	C	C
C	A	C	B	A	B
B	C	C	A	B	A
A	B	A	C	B	C
A	C	B	A	C	B

44

10	13	22	14	33	8	14	10
30	18	39	20	11	6	39	10
31	18	33	35	16	16	27	11
25	34	14	27	1	34	9	21
5	9	10	7	34	19	8	22
15	13	38	37	9	24	10	3
22	20	33	4	36	13	19	40
24	36	28	32	38	15	9	6

45

Solutions

46

The value of the central letter is the total value of the letter in the top right corner plus that in the bottom left corner, also that of the value of the letter in the top left corner plus that in the bottom right corner. Thus the missing value is 15, so the missing letter is O.

47

A – The top and bottom rows and the left and right columns all add up to the number in the central square.

48

2785

49

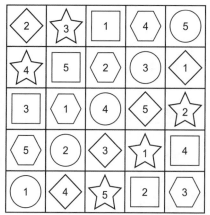

Solutions

50

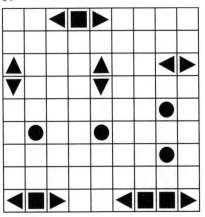

51

A

52

5	3	1	2	4	6
4	5	3	1	6	2
2	6	5	3	1	4
1	4	6	5	2	3
3	2	4	6	5	1
6	1	2	4	3	5

53

C5

54

Solutions

55

●	3	●	3	2	1		●		1
●			●	●				2	●
		1		●	5	●		3	3
	0	0		●	●			●	●
		1			2		1		
2		●	1					1	
●	●				0	1	●		
4				2			3	●	2
●	●	3	●	●				●	2
3	●		2		1			●	2

56

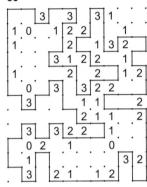

57

8 – Multiply the quantities in scale A by four, so that 4 hearts + 4 spades = 8 clubs, then replace these 4 hearts with their value in scale B, ie 1 club and 1 spade; so 1 club + 1 spade + 4 spades = 8 clubs. Thus 5 spades = 7 clubs. Now multiply the quantities in scale B by seven, so that 7 clubs + 7 spades = 28 hearts, then replace these 7 clubs with 5 spades (above). Thus (7 spades + 5 spades) 12 spades = 28 hearts. So 3 spades = 7 hearts. Scale C has 7 clubs (the same as 5 spades, above) + 7 hearts (the same as 3 spades, above), so 8 spades are needed to balance scale C.

Solutions

58

F	E	B	A	D	C
D	C	F	B	A	E
A	F	D	E	C	B
E	B	A	C	F	D
C	A	E	D	B	F
B	D	C	F	E	A

59

60

3	1	1	1	1	4
2	2	2	4	4	2
2	2	2	4	4	2
3	3	3	1	1	2
3	3	3	1	1	2
2	1	1	4	4	4

Solutions

61

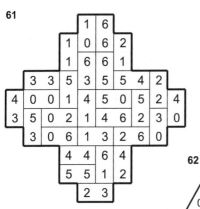

62

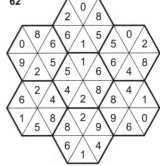

63

A	B	C	B	A	C
C	A	A	B	C	B
A	C	B	A	B	C
B	C	A	C	B	A
C	B	B	A	C	A
B	A	C	C	A	B

64

22	9	40	37	37	9	34	7
39	2	31	18	36	37	36	8
38	39	8	8	2	30	30	19
35	22	10	27	7	7	34	16
24	29	1	38	38	6	27	10
6	31	2	9	12	21	40	39
30	14	16	27	25	39	2	18
38	7	35	8	12	24	20	31

65

■	◆		▲		●
◆	●	■			▲
●		▲	■	◆	
		●	◆	▲	■
▲	■			●	◆
	▲	◆	●	■	

Solutions

66

The value of the central letter is the total value of the two letters in the furthest left boxes multiplied by the total value of the two letters in the furthest right boxes. Thus the missing value is 4, so the missing letter is D.

67

C – The totals of the left and right columns when subtracted from the totals of the top and bottom rows gives the number in the central square.

68

7783

69

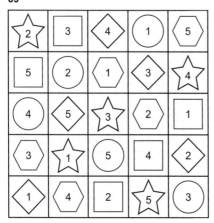

Solutions

70

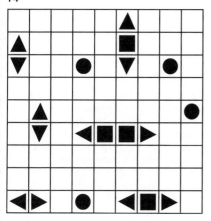

71
E

72

6	2	1	4	3	5
1	4	5	2	6	3
4	6	3	1	5	2
3	5	4	6	2	1
2	3	6	5	1	4
5	1	2	3	4	6

73
B6

74

Solutions

75

		0			0		●	
0						1		0
			2		1	0		
	3	●	●				●	
●	●	●	●	●	3		2	2
	5			3	●	1		●
●	2	●	1				●	4
	5				●	●	●	●
●	●	●	1	3	●		4	4
	3				●	2		●

76

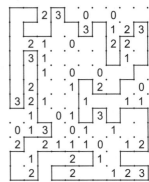

77

3 – Multiply the quantities in scale B by three, so that 3 diamonds + 6 hearts = 9 spades. Now replace these 6 hearts with their value in scale A, so that 1 diamond + 1 spade + 3 diamonds = 9 spades. Thus 4 diamonds = 8 spades, so 2 diamonds = 4 spades and 1 diamond = 2 spades. Now multiply the quantities in scale A by two, so that 2 diamonds + 2 spades = 12 hearts. Now replace these 2 spades with 1 diamond (above), so that 2 diamonds + 1 diamond = 12 hearts, so 1 diamond = 4 hearts. There are 4 spades (the same as 2 diamonds, above) and 4 hearts (the same as 1 diamond (above) in scale C. So a total of 3 diamonds are needed to balance scale C.

Solutions

78

E	F	B	A	D	C
F	A	D	C	B	E
B	C	A	F	E	D
C	D	E	B	F	A
A	E	F	D	C	B
D	B	C	E	A	F

79

80

1	3	3	3	3	2
2	4	4	1	1	1
2	4	4	1	1	1
1	3	3	2	2	4
1	3	3	2	2	4
3	2	2	3	3	3

Solutions

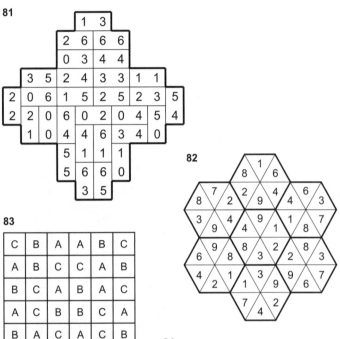

81

		1	3						
	2	6	6	6					
	0	3	4	4					
3	5	2	4	3	3	1	1		
2	0	6	1	5	2	5	2	3	5
2	2	0	6	0	2	0	4	5	4
	1	0	4	4	6	3	4	0	
		5	1	1	1				
		5	6	6	0				
		3	5						

82

83

C	B	A	A	B	C
A	B	C	C	A	B
B	C	A	B	A	C
A	C	B	B	C	A
B	A	C	A	C	B
C	A	B	C	B	A

84

9	15	26	18	4	18	9	26
34	34	23	12	19	9	30	35
27	33	25	24	39	39	17	8
14	36	13	12	34	29	38	13
15	2	3	31	27	38	3	6
30	7	34	13	24	18	7	34
4	3	12	23	24	11	18	9
37	33	38	12	20	4	7	35

85

Solutions

86

The value of the central letter is the total value of the letters in the top left, bottom left and bottom right squares, minus the value of the letter in the top right square. Thus the missing value is 17, so the missing letter is Q.

87

A – The letters are given numerical values according to their positions in the alphabet. These values, together with the number in the central square, are all prime numbers.

88

3553

89

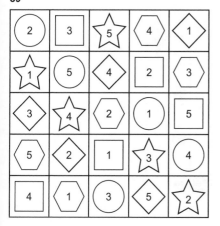

Solutions

90

91

B

92

6	5	2	4	3	1
4	6	1	3	5	2
3	1	5	6	2	4
1	2	4	5	6	3
2	3	6	1	4	5
5	4	3	2	1	6

93

F7

94

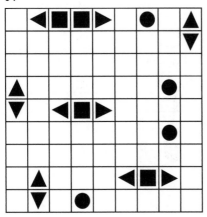

Solutions

95

●	3	●	●		●	1			●
		●	4	2	1		1	2	
	2	●	2		1	1		●	2
1					●	2	2	3	●
	●	●	●	3		●			●
1		3		●	3	1		2	2
		1	2	●			2	●	1
●	●	1				●		1	
4		3			1				1
●	●	●		0			1	●	

96

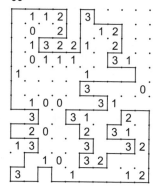

97

16 – Multiply the quantities in scale B by five, so that 5 clubs + 10 hearts = 20 spades. Now replace the 5 clubs in scale B with their value in scale A, so that 12 hearts = 14 spades, thus 6 hearts = 7 spades, and 36 hearts = 42 spades. Multiply scale A by seven, so that 14 hearts + 42 spades = 35 clubs. Now replace these 42 spades with 36 hearts, so that 14 hearts + 36 hearts = 35 clubs, thus 50 hearts = 35 clubs. So 10 hearts = 7 clubs. there are 7 spades (the same as 6 hearts, above) and 7 clubs (the same as 10 hearts, above) in scale C. Thus a total of 16 hearts are needed to balance scale C.

Solutions

98

B	F	D	A	E	C
C	B	F	E	D	A
E	A	C	B	F	D
D	C	E	F	A	B
A	E	B	D	C	F
F	D	A	C	B	E

99

100

1	4	4	2	2	1
2	4	4	3	3	1
2	4	4	3	3	1
2	2	2	3	3	2
2	2	2	3	3	2
1	2	2	1	1	4